Smart

Money

50 Tips on How to achieve Financial Success and the Mindset it takes to get there.

By Jeff Heldrich

Examine This Book on Kindle
For A Full 7 Days

100% Risk FREE!

That's right… If you are not 110% satisfied, you have seven days to go to "Manage Your Kindle" page and ask for a complete Refund!

Be sure to checkout my other book **"Mind Power"** if you are looking to improve your life in other aspects outside of personal finance!

FOREWARD

In America and most countries, personal finance has not yet become a required learning subject in high school or college, so the average person might be fairly clueless as to how to manage and spend your money intelligently when you're out in the real world for the first time.

Regardless of your economic situation, getting your finances in order is a good thing to do at any time of year, no matter when you do begin. To help you get started, this book will focus on the 50 most important things to understand about personal finance and break it down in the most simple steps possible.

Be prepared to feel at ease once you your money is in order, and you time on the more important things in life knowing you will be financially ready for when hard times arrive.

CONTENTS

CHAPTER 1:
BUDGETING

Unfortunately, people consider budgeting as a way of being stingy with money, and it's one of the reasons most people keep-off from it as if they were dieting. The same way dieting works as a scheme for moderating how to eat and what to eat, budgeting is also a program for moderating how to spend and what to spend on. Well if the name "budgeting" has a bad connotation for you, you can try another suitable name like "personal financial planning" and that is exactly what it means, nothing more or less. Budgeting is more of a proactive action, not a reactionary one and has nothing to do with your education with finance, whether you are a university under-graduate, degree holder or you are a retiree.

Whether your cutting costs because you need to or want to, the process should be manageable and positive. Either you are a master of your money or a slave to it. These tips can help reduce your spending without making major sacrifices or time commitments

Get your money automated

You can make your finance system trouble-free and painless to if it is automated; automating your money is a good way of discharging money directly to your other accounts where it can be secured and dispersible, this way, you can easily manage how money flows out and how it flows into your account.

You can equally decide to program your finance system in a way that, your money will be controlled from the paycheck to the retirement savings account, or using it to pay bills such as cable and internet. By automating your funds, you can reduce the rate of moving money around; it upgrades your account and make it function automatically.

The Importance of Liquidity

In advent of an emergency or crises, the importance of liquid assets comes to fore as they can be converted to cash easily. If not for liquidity, your money can be stuck in a financial structure where it would be hard for you to cash it or even more difficult to access for real cash value. Liquid assets are important in periods of crises or emergency because they are easily converted to cash. In these times big financial institutions may become non-functional, which makes it a hard task to access cash to purchase essentials such as food, household utilities and other emergency needs.

Making expenses which we did not plan for are normal. Repairs, hospital bills, insurance deductibles, utility bills - these are all expected debt issues if you fail to keep a contingency fund.

You may also avoid reliance on credit card debt with high-interest rate when emergencies come up by having a separate bank account with funds which are equal to three to six months expenses and that are easily accessible.

Keep away from any account maintenance fees

Some banks charge annual or monthly maintenance fees, the normal monthly maintenance fee for the average American bank is around $12. Carefully discover the fee your bank charges you every month for account maintenance and see if you can figure a way to stop it. Check if it can be waived or suspended, some banks do allow a waive if your are able to keep up with a certain minimum daily balance. Get acquainted with your bank's policy to know if you are charged and figure out ways of avoiding it.

Carefully look out for any other hidden bank charges

More often we ignore the minor sneaky bank fees and rather focus on the majors like ATM charges, maintenance charges and of course overdraft fees, which are more rewarding for the banks, but it's important you stay alert on other ways your bank might want to exploit you, these sort of fees might not mean so much but they add up, things to look our for include; the check-cashing fees, return deposit fees, wire transfer charges, excess transaction charges, paper statement charges, minimum balance fees, including foreign operation charges, these are little ways your bank can drain money out of you.

But, you do have the right to question the management and complain about any fee you were charged unjustly, and see if that helps you get a refund. This would be a lot easier if you have more than one account with the bank. Banks will count you as a more valuable customer and likely would try to keep you satisfied by cutting down some minor charges.

It's never too late to get a financial adviser

Overtime, I have learned there is no financial problem that is too much or too little to solve. Be reminded that hiring a financial adviser is a huge investment, because the decision you take in managing your wealth can either make or break your assets.

Below are some circumstances that might require you to hire a financial planner. Financial planners charge between $100 to $500 fee per hour, it might seem expensive. but I assures you it is not a waste. After you're married or divorced - When you get into marriage or you are getting a divorce. The planner will assist you on how to set your financial record back on track after possible losses in the wedding or court charges you went through. He will be also able to teach you ways of harmonizing your income so that family needs don't outweigh your financial capacity.

When you don't earn much or save much or if you are at a point of low earnings, an advisor will lecture you on how to manage money no matter how small, whether you want to finance your children's education fees, save against retirement, buy a house or a car. You need a nest egg for the future in order to achieve that, the financial planning process will help you identify how much you will need to save over time.

We all have heard the stories of how some trust fund babies or lottery winners became broke all of a sudden, that's because managing big money requires good mentoring, the trick to sustaining wealth is often harder than acquiring it. A financial planner helps you plan your money and assist you on classic mistakes such as living beyond your means or constantly gifting for families and friends.

Be on the lookout for opportunities

We all have worked hard, going the extra mile, dreaming big but yet we get only lemons from life. Some people overlook these lemons, going for what we feel we deserve even if it is far beyond our capacity. The result is huge pile of debt or zero savings for retirement. In actual fact, what we are actually doing is selling our future stability, financial freedom and independence for temporary pleasure.

One thing is certain, we all deserve a better life, a better car and house, vacations and so much more.

But it is important for us to spend our money wisely to avoid these problems and pay the price in the future. There is time for everything. If we fail to observe this simple rule, we will end up spending our money now without leaving some to take on opportunities that will show up in the future.

Create a Budget to cover Impulsive buying

It isn't easy for some of us to easily turn our eyes away from an object we so desire. This could be because we may never get the opportunity again to buy the object again. The best thing is not to fight impulsive buying, but to accommodate in what is referred to as splurge budget.

A splurge budget does exactly what its name implies; the money you set aside from your income to buy things you were not really prepared for. Nothing says you must spend it, but once it is spent; don't go looking for it again. Though it may seem you are encouraging yourself to indulge in impulsive spending by creating a splurge budget, in actual truth, you are enhancing your budgeting skills.

Use just a little part of your available credit

To keep things safe, keep it at 25%. When trying to get a premium score, then your best bet is to keep things as low as possible.

In previous years, consumers were advised by credit counselors to have their dormant accounts closed when applying for a mortgage or a vehicle. Their rationale was that people who were too lose with their spending and could easily max out their credit card.

However, you won't be penalized by FICO score if you end up with huge credit unspent. The amount of credit you have available will be compared on the amount you have actually spent based on most credit scoring model. Your score will plummet if the percentage venture is high. If you decide to immediately close your account, your available credit will drop, while your debt will still be high.

Putting money into savings

No one enjoys being caught off guard financially. However the truth is that you will at some point be confronted with a financial emergency which can take the form of home repair, car repair, or medical bills. It is important you keep money aside for financial emergency, but this amount varies for each individual. For starters, you should set aside six months of expenses or even more.

Finance experts recommend keeping nine months to one year worth of expenses into savings. Individuals with families, who rely on one source of income, or depend on commissions should leave nothing less than one year of their expenses into their savings. Though using credit cards to fund financial emergencies may seem like a viable option, it is often a temporary solution as you will still have to pay them back plus an added interest.

No matter how tight your budget may seem, there is always room for you to take out from it and build up a safety nest you can go to when you discover your income flow has ceased. Expenses like loans or payment of a credit card need to be taken into account when making your calculations.

You are almost half done when you succeed in putting 3 months of your expenditures into savings. But you don't have to stop there, Save up as much as you can, as doing so gives you some form of financial security. Imagine the freedom that comes from knowing that you barely have to worry about money again.

Have a monthly saving plan

After deciding the amount of money you want to save up, next is to create a monthly plan to reach that goal. If your plan is to save up for a new car, you can start by putting away $200 into savings every month.

You can use several strategies in developing your saving plan. To avoid ditching the plan in the first week, ensure the plan is a reasonable one which you can stick to. For instance, trying to save money by cutting out every form of recreational expenses only sets you up for failure. Another efficient technique is to have a portion of your monthly income stashed up into your savings account the moment you receive your check.

Never relent in paying off your loan

What are your plans for paying off the loan on your car? It is important to set money aside every month to offset the loan, but you will have to make the payments yourself.

This is an efficient saving technique, as you have cultivated the habit of making monthly installments on the loan you have borrowed. If you have no plans of going for another loan soon, then having your money put into an investment account won't be much of a problem.

See the Money You've Saved

A good amount of millennials get hit with large expenses, or find themselves needing money for food or consumables, and break into their savings just as they've begun to build it up. This is a bad habit; one that's hard to break. That's why it's best to store your savings in an account that you don't have quick access to (checking or savings account), like a bank that makes you withdraw money in person.

One of the smartest ways to save money is to invest it in Blue Chip Stocks (best performing stocks as chosen by the Dow Jones Industrial and the S&P 500). You won't be able to access it quickly and you can grow your money at the same time.

CHAPTER 2:
SPENDING

Whether your cutting costs because you need to or want to, the process should be manageable and positive. Either you are a master of your money or a slave to it. These tips can help reduce your spending without making major sacrifices or time commitments

Have a Budget

Keep a concise record of all you have spent your money on for at least 2 months. When you have done this, next categorize your expenditures in food, entertainment etc. After completing this task, you will want to take into account your monthly bills, as doing so gives you a clear picture of your spending pattern. Your goal for developing a budget is to find ways of trimming down your expenditure, while also saving up a good part of your earnings.

Create a checklist out of your bills, and then make a comparison of it with your monthly income. Each bill you pay should be knocked off your checklist. Put a part of your monthly income to your savings. It is also advisable to put money into a vacation account if you plan on traveling, doing so provides you with money when you are in need of it. Any money that is left at the end of the month after covering up expenses, should either go into your savings or should be used to offset debt.

End every impulse purchase

Unplanned purchases are not very advisable to anyone who wants to invest rightly and grow wealth, learn to plan your buying, if at all you are having some habit problem in managing your income, you can confide in a trusted friend who can assist you with how to spend and when to spend, if you trust him/her enough, you can hand over your credit card or wallet to them and let them hold it far from your reach. This sounds totally crazy but it works wonders. With time, you will learn good money spending discipline.

The use of Credit Cards Snowballs the Amount of Money You Spend

It is an established fact that the use of credit cards for your daily transactions inevitably increase the total amount of money you spend. Spending with credit cards is often easy and exciting until you realize that it's not affordable. At that juncture, your spendings and interests are now owed to the bank. If you are familiar with this type of problem, then you will have to make a budget plan that will help you not spend money from credit cards anymore. Estimate your total monthly income and your required expenditures. Then the remaining ought to be used to settle your debts.

It is difficult to resist from fun habits such as entertainment and eating out, but this should be refrained from temporarily until your debt load is reduced. You have to be mindful of the big picture. Once you are done paying off your credit card, you can spend that money as you desire.

Avoid ATM Use

One way to prevent money loss is by avoiding ATMs owned by banks other than yours, in this scenario every time you make a transaction, you pay for it, you don't just pay the bank for the transaction, you equally pay your bank. I know this might not be very convenient but try not to pay attention to ATMs outside of your own bank network. To make this easy for you, research the locations of your banks ATMs or you can opt to choose a bank with a wide network of ATMs that waives the fees.

Never waste money

Money saved is as good as money earned. Resist the temptation of spontaneous spending on items you may not necessarily need. Instead of saying to your self "I saved $60 this month by staying away from doughnuts every morning", say "I earned $60 this month by resisting the temptation of buying doughnuts every morning". If you are thinking otherwise, consider the tremendous amount of effort it took you to resist the temptation. You went all the way to overcome a habit you are already used to and as a reward, you earned $60. If you smoke, consider the amount of money you would save if you could give up your smoking habit. The money you would have spent on these bad habits can then be used for bettering your life.

Cut out unnecessary insurance

As life keeps changing, your insurance changes alongside with it. You can start effecting changes starting with your car insurance. As your car ages, it makes sense for you ro increase its deductible so as to decrease premiums.

Also it is important you have sufficient cash to cover up for any accident that might occur.

Having the deductible on your car increased will definitely save you a lot in vehicle insurance every month.

Power Saving Appliances

Everything now requires energy to run, our home devices, work place installation facilities, etc, but there are still lot of measures we can take to save energy. We can cut down on some things to stop the bills from pilling up. There is really so much money we can save by simply making some necessary changes in power usage at home.

Below are some of those measures:

- Hack your laundry and dish washer

Every day as you use that washer, more energy is consumed and the bills cumulate. You can lessen that consumption rate and save some energy for yourself by using these tips.

Try using cold water when washing, especially for multicolor-clothes. You really do not have to change the way you operate your laundry machine, all you need do, is press another button, and it will work.

For dish washing, do not use high heat, always reduce it, you really do not need that high heat to have your dishes nicely washed, we all know that hot water kills the microbes and germs during the wash, but remember the machine has alternative options for a reason, use them in a way it will serve you better.

- Make use of CFL light bulbs

Compact Fluorescent Lights (CFLs) have a longer duration ability than incandescent bulbs. Also they reduce the flare of carbon IV oxide in air, using CFL light bulbs saves up to half-ton of carbon IV oxide from escaping into your environment which is safer than using incandescent bulbs.

You can save a lot of energy by just using CFL light bulb, its energy consumption rate is 50-80% less than that of the incandescent bulb, so if you are really interested in saving more energy, CFL light bulbs are ideal.

- Control the temperature of your refrigerator

Your freezer or refrigerator is another energy consuming beast. Of course you do not want warm temperature to spoil your food, but with the help of a thermometer, you can monitor your refrigerators temperature so it is ideal.

For your freezer, you can limit the temperature range to Fahrenheit 0 to 5 degrees, however changes can happen at any time, there are different temperature usages for winter and another for summer; you don't use hot temperature for hot weather and cold temperature for cold weather, that's why your thermometer is important.

Ensure the freezer door is sealed with the "dollar bill test". A door tightly sealed saves money as well, if the door is slippery and does not hold the bill, consider replacing it.

Killawattor

The killawattor is an effective mean of conserving energy, which helps you know how much energy your electronics consume.

This is best suited for computer device or microwaves, because it's easy to tell when they are on or off. However, it can be difficult for heavy energy consuming machines like the refrigerators, water cooler, pressing iron etc

Choose the right gas station

Some gas stations are better than others. Many grocery stores, department stores, and wholesale clubs offer gas lower than the price leaders or even at a loss for them, they do this in order to encourage people to shop at their stores, where they can make up that loss in sales of groceries and other items. Most of these places require a membership, and some give you credit for in-store purchase when you fill up your tank. There are a lot of factors to consider, but in the end you might save a lot of money picking a station like this over the price leaders in your area. Service stations usually offer gas at a higher price than others.

Drive slow and steady to save money

We all have a need for speed, but reving your engine and driving high miles increases your gas consumption by a lot. If you're the type who enjoys speeding by cars in the passing lane, and your RMP is always on the red zone whenever you are in the driver's seat, think again. You can decrease your fuel consumption by two miles a gallon, and with over a full years worth, it adds up to quite a lot of money saved.

You can also save a couple hundred dollars annually by pumping gas yourself and ensuring you are using the lowest octane you can for your car. A well-tuned engine and the right tire pressure means your gas consumption won't be nearly as high.

Know what it costs to repair your car

There are a variety of websites that can give you a general idea as to how much a repair on your car costs: AutoMD.com and RepairPal.com. Sites like these give you fair estimates on repairs where you live; often ranging from the lowest price to the highest. Normally, a fair price is somewhere in between. Make sure to fully read your car manual so as to avoid causing any damages to your car in the first place.

Record Keeping

Keeping well-detailed business records is vital. These records give you insight into how profitable your business is, it helps you avoid problems with tax authorities down the line, it also protects you from lawsuits, and helps you build and maintain relationships with vendors and clientele, it can also aid you in winning a lawsuit if you're harmed. There are however, requirements and laws as to how to properly keep records and how long to keep those records. Which requirements apply to you is wholly dependent on your business. That said, some records should be kept by all businesses. We will talk about the more important ones here.

The records needed for tax and accounting purposes are:

- Check stubs
- Credit card statements
- Income
- Bank statements
- Business expenses
- Annual tax returns
- Payroll
- Sales
- Travel log
- Petty cash
- Credit card sales receipts
- Vehicle use log
- Cash register tapes
- Quarterly tax filings
- Invoices
- Canceled checks
- Inventory

Other Important Records

This is not the end-all, be-all list, and we want to reiterate that the kind of records you need are dependent on your business type. However, these are a few other records you will want to keep.

- Trademark registrations and patents
- Personnel records
- Articles of incorporation
- Inventory logs
- Permits

- Accident reports
- Licenses
- Purchase orders

There's an old saying: you get what you pay for. Buying cheap insurance usually means buying the bare minimum allowed by the law. You may save today, but if you're in an accident, you may not be able to repair or replace your car. That means paying hundreds, even thousands of dollars out of pocket if you have an insurance claim, which is a lot more than you saved with your cheap car insurance.

Don't go for cheap, go for quality. Determine what sort of coverage you will need and shop around. Compare prices; Progressive has a tool called Coverage Checker, which lets you compare rates easily. You can also get in touch with an independent agent. Whatever choice you make, make sure you get the right coverage.

Spend a Little, Save a Lot

Utilities cost money. It's a simple truth, which is why you should weatherize your property today. You can call your utility company and demand an audit, or look for a certified contractor that can provide you with a total home energy efficiency review. You may find that you only need low-cost, simple improvements like sealing doors and windows, or more costly improvements like installing insulation. However, you will save thousands of dollars on your utilities.

CHAPTER 3:
MISTAKES TO AVOID

Lets take a look at the most common mistakes people make with their money. Which often makes people fall into a financial crisis. If you are already in a financial rut, avoiding these mistakes at all costs will be key to your survival.

Focus on reflexive and residual earnings

Wealth is hardly gotten by wage based jobs, it's like trading your time with money, if you want to achieve financial freedom, you have to build a system that will constantly generate wealth, this is known as making your money work for you and not working for money.

Wealthy people focus on passive and consistent income rather than active but inconsistent income, because that's where they can get paid more for their investment on that field.

It's not enough to work-hard, if you are working hard, you must work smart, that's what makes your work productive, there are many fields you can smartly use to generate more money, such as doing an online business, investing in big lucrative business firms or buying shares, writing books etc. Check out freelancer websites like upwork.com or elance.com to find people who would be glad to help you out in just about any field and at a great price.

Manage your time intelligently

Time management plays a major role in our income earnings, but it's one thing to spend time and another thing to invest time, the more time you invest can give you more money, instead of using that time to play around watching TV shows after work, you can invest that time into something that will work for you in your sleep.

Let's say you want a new earnings milestone for your business. Use the extra time you have to have develop and build what is require to take that business to the next level, and start putting that as your main priority.

Or maybe you are a job seeker who has been sending thousands of resumes to different sites and hoping luck can catch up with you someday to land that high paying job. But on the other hand, you can invest that same time on researching great companies and find a job you are really passionate about, and focusing on writing a job application that will make you stand out above everyone else. Now these two scenarios play out into the same prospect, but the latter approach is much less commonly used and is a better strategy that has more chances of getting the positive result.

Don't rely on a shortcut to success

Shortcuts usually sound fascinating from the outside. However the situation in real life is quiet different from the fictional depictions. Let us imagine that there is no shortcut to success in life and everybody gets rewarded according to how diligent they are about work. If that were the case, that means Bill Gates who makes around $11 billion per year ($13 million per hour) would have to work fifty-four thousand times harder than an average American who earns $50,000 annually.

All of us want to believe that hard work is rewarding. Yes, it is. However, your hard work reaches a stage where it cannot increase. You cannot have more than 24 hours in a day. So there is a limit to the work you can do. What you can instead do is to learn how to work smarter. Instead of trying so hard to accomplish everything at once, just pick one or two important goals and exert all of your effort and focus on them. It is better to have one very successful accomplishment than a lot of mediocre and disappointing trials.

Never hesitate when the impulse is present

Dreams become goals when they have been seized, written down and courageously planned. Goals remain dormant if action is not taken, you must determine to pursue your goal to the tee. Make out time every day to work on that goal, as long as you are planting an effort daily, it doesn't matter how long it takes but you will see progress eventually

Make Opportunities your focal point

A lot of times, we put so much energy trying to make the most put of our career and goals and don't expect that life or the economy will throw stones back at us, some of which have knocked people out of their dreams, they include, stones of frustration, stones of discouragement or even stones of financial troubles, but if we listen to those inner fears, we might miss the right opportunity. Adapt an attitude of not paying attention to those throwbacks; navigate your attention to your goal and drive it through your plans, not through the distractions along the way or what you hear.

Learn how to take smart risks

If you tell someone you wish to go out on a date with (if it doesn't work out, the worst you can get is an open embarrassment, but if it works out, good, you may be dancing along in a relationship with a soul mate) Or asking your boss for a promotion (if it turns out wrong, your boss will say "No", but if it turns out well, he will give you a permanent promotion and better salary)

Create a blog (the worst thing that can come out of it, is a bunch of wasted time, best case scenario, it generates more income to you can possibly make a full time income talking about your passion)

Wake up and take action where you can, if you don't you will always regret not realizing your full potential.

Try to get a good credit report

The earlier you get your credit improved, the better; it takes several months to have any error on a credit report sorted out. Scrutinize it properly before applying for a car loan or mortgage with it. Never hesitate to contact the credit bureau the moment you spot errors, like incorrect balance or a payment which indicates you missed it when you actually paid it. When making your claims, take documents with you that will make your claims more valid.

Have a will

A will helps put your finances in order long after you are gone. No one likes the idea of dying, but death is an unavoidable price every one of us will have to pay one day. If you fail to put down a will before your demise, then the government will have to act on Intestacy Rule in determining what happens to your money and valuables you left behind.

Your family members will find it easy to put your affairs in order after you are gone, if you left a will. Without a will, all the possessions and money you have will be shared based on the law, which of course nobody likes. If you have a will, the tax that will be placed on your property or money you left behind will be less. A will is very important especially if you have relatives and children who depend on you for their financial needs, or you want someone outside your immediate family to get a portion of your money.

Customers don't always know what they want

If you are a young entrepreneur, and you are seeking to grow in your business, you need to figure out what's best for your brand by yourself and not what your customers think, many entrepreneurs make the mistake of asking customers what they want, but really customers don't know what they want, you are the one who is responsible for filtering them something they want, even if they didn't know about it before.

Even if you want to get feedback from your customers, you have to initiate your product first before seeking for extra help on how to improve on it. This can equally help you survive in the competitive business society, because every customer has one or two things that are constantly attracting him/her to the product.

You have to first figure out what you are going to create and then get feedback from customers after it's created. Just like in the printing business, new printers didn't just emerge, they started coming up the moment Laser printer was created, competition did not see this innovation coming and neither did the customers.

Listen to your audience

I know it seems contradictive given the last topic. However when you a starting a business it can be hard to know when you are producing a defective product, likewise when a movie director producing a bad movie. There are times we come up with killer ideas that we believe are a masterpiece, only to realize that others aren't too impressed about our work. It sends our morale plummeting, but this is part of the law of business and you have no choice but to adapt. It is always best to pay attention to what your audience really wants, instead of trying to prove a point or comfort your ego.

Risk Intelligently

Great successful corporations are defined by the risk they take, any establishment that mentors on risk taking will always have an expansion tendency, risk differentiates growing organizations from lagging organizations. The more you inspire and motivate your staff on the idea of taking well calculated actions coupled with risk, the more they learn new ways of making progress.

In as much as risk taking is vital in organizational growth, it is also stupid to take dumb impulsive risks, you must study the relevant risk management system appropriate for your business and understand the environment.

Fear of the unknown makes people run away from risk taking because they already see failure in their journey, and assume they are a candidate to fail. Negative perception shouldn't hinder you from making the decision, even if you try and fail, it's a learned and invaluable experience.

Never fall for the trap of "Credit Scams"

One good way of staying away from debt is to avoid credit counseling scams or credit repair altogether. Companies have been relentless in trying to capture the attention of customers with poor credit history; offering to help them get rid of the debt overnight so as to enable them access a car loan or home mortgage. In truth, these companies will literally do nothing, to disappear into thin air after sifting hundreds or thousands of dollars from their ignorant victims. The bitter truth is that at the end of the day, it is this unscrupulous set of individuals that will have their finances improved, while the consumers themselves are left in a terrible financial shape, most times sinking deeper into the debt they were trying to get out of. Here are tips that can help you steer clear of these dubious schemes;

- Be highly speculative if a company asks you to pay before any work will be done
- Being instructed not to contact credit reporting companies like TransUnion, Experian and Equifax. Never hesitate to get a hold of them when you have issues with your credit.
- They tell you to supply incorrect information when applying for credit
- As a rule of thumb, stay away from non-profit credit counseling companies

Use smaller milestones in reaching your financial goals

For instance, you have plans of raising $50,000 for your business through your personal savings. Instead of using this huge sum as a goal, the best thing to do is to break it down. If you have plans of saving up $50,000 this year, then you goal should be to save $400 every month, and $87.5 every week.

Breaking your financial goals into small milestones clarifies your goal, It is easy to convince yourself to save $87.5 this week, than convincing yourself to save $50,000 in the next five years.

Avoid cosigning a loan

If your friend has fallen into bad debt, it is likely s/he will come to you to co-sign their loan so as to get approval. Before penning down your signature, it is important you clearly understand what you are getting into.

Most times, a company that needs an individual to get their loan request cosigned is a sign that they have very little trust in the borrower. It is only in few circumstances that this is advisable. Such circumstances include cosigning a child's student loan, or setting a up a young person to receive their first credit card. The truth is that you have nothing to gain but all to lose when cosigning a loan.

Though you might have cosigned a car loan you aren't driving, or the mortgage for a house you aren't living in, they are all part of your liability. Your credit score will only improve a tiny bit based on your monthly payments. You have little need for extra credit line since your good credit has qualified you as a co-signer. Co-signing a loan puts you at the risk of repaying the loan if it ends up not being paid, while your credit score can only improve a little.

Avoid Overdraft fees

Overdraft fees are between about $10 and $35, depending on your bank, which means just one overdraft monthly could cost you $100 to $420 annually. The more you are familiar with the pros and cons of these charges, the better you are at managing your cash. By putting your spending habits into consideration, you will be able to figure what method can be best used to avoid overdraft fees.

CHAPTER 4:
SUCCESFUL MINDSET

While growing your financial portfolio, there will be times when you appear more confident than you actually feel. On the outside you appear confident, while inside you have some doubt and worry about the steps you are taking. Your thoughts and feelings determine your actions; a positive mindset sets you up for success.

The secret to success is thinking big

Thinking big opens your mind to unlimited possibilities which you can turn into reality. When you think big, you see opportunities where others see limitations and you become a more positive person.

Negative or fearful thinking is the enemy of big thinking. Never use the word "impossible" in your communication. While successful people see reasons as to why they can, unproductive people only see reasons why they can't. Successful people see any problem that comes along their way as a challenge and an opportunity. This is because their big thinking empowers them to see solutions where every other person sees limitations. You just have to be optimistic and courageous, seizing every opportunity that comes to you in form of a challenge.

Associate yourself with the rich

If your money is limited, then it's not a good idea to live beyond your means or throw it around. If you notice, money is hardly lost through frivolous spending, but due rather to bad business decisions.

One single bad business move can wreck you financially beyond recovery. You reduce this scenario by surrounding yourself with wealthy friends that have already made these mistakes. This is what smart entrepreneurs have always done. Having the right set of friends helps you grow financially because they will ensure you don't lose money carelessly even when you don't realize you are.

Make accountability exhilarating

It's obvious people bring out their best when they are accountable to others, such as when they have a boss they who pushes them to meet a target. Other people tend to work better under the pressure of meeting up with deadlines.

The thing with these motivating factors is that it puts people under tension and they become consumed with fear of not producing good results. You have to pledge your commitment and effort, regardless of the circumstance, a lot of times we encounter challenges that make us deny sticking with commitments, they can create distraction between you and your goal but don't let that limit you, see your achieving that goal as your only option and seize it.

Increase the amount of time you spend on your job

Time is money. Sitting all day watching daytime TV will definitely not add a dime to your pocket. But putting more efforts into your job will definitely build you up financially. If your place of work is just a stone throw from your place of residence, then buying a car only builds up your liability.

Moving closer your job betters you financially. There may be need to effect some changes. Switching to a job that takes just an hour from you when commuting, from one that takes three hours when commuting, will definitely improve your work-life balance.

At the end of day, you would have saved 522 hours/year in your car. This is about 40 hours worth of work weeks.

Stay Positive and visualize

Make it a habit to jot down the positive things about your business, then recite them daily and begin to live in that consciousness. Re-program what you viewed in the past, and see past the average person, envision yourself in that high position you are working for. If you have a bad impression of rich people, than repeat a mantra like "Rich people are ambitious, hardworking and dedicated people. I strive to reach such a level of accomplishment one day.

Remember you can't be rich by shunning rich-life, it's something you should desire and be prepared for. You must begin to see yourself as that rich person, if writing about your aspirations and posting them on the wall can help you focus on that experience, then fine. Use your affirmation to create that reality, you can use pictures of private jets, luxurious houses and wealthy people, use just about anything that makes you feel motivated.

Stay Optimistic as a Goal Getter

Attitude is powerful in the business of achieving goals, cultivate a optimistic attitude, let your imagination be positive and focused on achieving that big dream, don't always panic or criticize, see the good side of that ugly situation and harness on that. Encourage yourself every day with posts and comments that will push you to dream bigger and as you make progress, record them and continue. By so doing, your success will begin to emerge before your very eyes and you will stand to rejoice every moment of your life. You have an amazing business life if you direct your thoughts and attitude to an angle where it will favor your business. Now it's in your hand to champion progress in that goal, step up your mentality and embrace your aspirations.

See Beyond the Obstacles

People are afraid of failing and wouldn't want to risk a fail at the end of the day, but the question is, how do you see your goal? Are you seeing inevitable challenges and failures in it or are you seeing beyond the boundary walls? Understand that your success largely depends on the way you perceive your goals and until you begin to see the good and bad side of that goal, you adapt a realistic mindset to make it work. The secret of greatness knowing your obstacles and overcoming them.

Rise above your mistakes

It's not worth it to dwell on your mistakes, they happen, some are even unavoidable. The best way out is to try to learn from your mistakes not to wallow and ponder on them, every mistake has the tendency to attract setbacks or upgrade. Instead of allowing the mistake grow, why not listen to the voice of your audience, understand the fault they discovered in your delivery and figure out a way to fix it, that's how to rise above such a challenge.

Thumb sucking never helps

Get yourself busy with research that will produce information which will draw you closer to that goal, it's wise to seek a friend who will keep you on check to ensure you are meeting the target. The secret to Warren Buffet's wealth is high ability to arrive at a decision and acting quickly upon it. He describes dilly dallying as thumb sucking. When trying to make a business decision, he instantly makes a decision the moment he has been provided with a good price before anyone else does, every bit of time you spend pondering unnecessarily is a lost opportunity to generate income.

Residual or passive income should be your main focus

You have very limited time each day and that is why it will be difficult for you to build wealth when you spend a good amount of your time working for money. People that built financial success know how to make more money by making their money work for them.

Your money gets to work for you when you put it into real estate, investments, publishing a book and other examples where you put work into something once, and the income becomes passive over time. If you are the one doing the work, your efforts have to be rewarded by none other than yourself. It's okay to work hard, but it's even better to work smarter.

Massive action taking

Finally know that goals and dreams can only be captured when deliberate planned actions are taken. Action puts you closer to success. Do something every day that will bring you closer to your dreams.

Big thinkers are optimistic set of people. Your attitude determines your growth. Never complain or criticize anyone. No matter how bad a thing may be, there is always a good to it; look for it. Be positive about yourself, depend on it knowing it will make you progress. Have a journal where you enter your daily progress. Celebrate your small wins, and then watch how your overall progress improves. Once you change your thinking and habit, every other thing about you will be changed in a positive way.

Be sure to Checkout my other book
"**Mind Power**" if you are looking to
improve your life in other aspects
outside of personal finance!

Thanks for reading! If you enjoyed this book or found it useful I'd be very grateful if you'd post a short review on Amazon. Your support really does make a difference and I read all the reviews personally so I can get your feedback and make this book even better.

Thanks again for your support!

CONCLUSION

There you have it! Apply yourself and you will be on your way to great financial success! Be prepared to accomplish your dreams and discover potential you thought you never had! Thank you for taking the time to read my book and stay tuned for more books on financial success in the future.

www.ingramcontent.com/pod-product-compliance
Lightning Source LLC
Chambersburg PA
CBHW051822170526
45167CB00005B/2116